1) 5 differences

HINT:
Differences can come from either picture. Two hints are provided in this first puzzle.

2) 5 differences

3) *5 differences*

4) 5 differences

5) 5 differences

6) 5 differences

7) 5 differences

8) 5 differences

9) 5 differences

10) 6 differences

11) 6 differences

12) 6 differences

13) 6 differences

14) 6 differences

15) 6 differences

16) 6 differences

17) 6 differences

18) 6 differences

19) 6 differences

20) 7 differences

21) 7 differences

22) 7 differences

23) 7 differences

24) 7 differences

25) 7 differences

26) 7 differences

27) 7 differences

28 **7 differences**

29) 7 differences

[redacted] 7 differences

7 differences

32) 7 differences

33) 10 differences

34) 10 differences

35) 10 differences

36) 10 differences

37) 10 differences

38) 10 differences

1)

2)

3)

4)

5)

6)

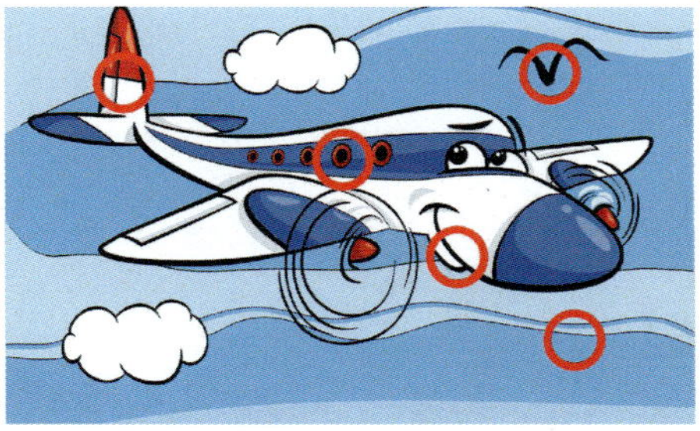

7)

8)

9)

10)

11)

12)

13)

14)

15)

16)

17)

18)

19)

20)

21)

22)

23)

24)

25)

26)

27)

28)

29)

30)

31)

32)

33)

34)

35)

36)

37)

38)

Manufactured by Amazon.ca
Bolton, ON

29503761R00026